PENDULUM SWINGS

Small Group Bible Study

Based on the film "Pendulum Swings"

A Bill Rahn film

www.pendulumswingsmovie.com

FILM SYNOPSIS

PENDULUM SWINGS follows a man into a dark place in his life; a place at which he arrives through a combination of bad decisions and forces beyond his control. When he finally hits bottom, he is presented with an opportunity to climb out of his despair – with a helping hand from a small number of people who could have chosen to judge him or write him off, but choose instead to offer compassion and grace. For our desperate character, the decision is ultimately his own – and when the pendulum does eventually swing back, his new life throws up a whole new set of challenges and choices.

PREFACE

Each week this Study Guide will provide you with a movie clip and four simple sections to help you facilitate a successful small group. The DVD clip will be played during the weekly small group time, so look for the movie clip icon below to play it at the right time.

Throughout this Small Group Study, we hope to help you look at some real life issues through the eyes of others. Maybe you will view the world from a new and different perspective.

www.pendulumswingsmovie.com

Printed in the USA

Cover Design by *Josh McDowell*

Photos by *Dan McDilda*

Authors: Bill Carrier, Victor and Charity Gray, John Keogh, Jennifer Rahn, Josh McDowell, Mary Reid, Robbie Starnes, Bob Templeton, and Paul Withrow.

Managing Author – Josh McDowell

Technical Editor – Jennifer Rahn

Producer – Bill Rahn

Table of Contents

CHAPTER 1

It Was a Play?

By Josh McDowell

It Was a Play?

Movie Connection

Show movie clip #1 on Group DVD

"And cut!" What? Were you surprised by the realization that you were watching a movie filmed within the actual movie?

I know I was shocked while reading the script for the first time. But immediately, the thought hit me: How many people would be surprised if they could back up and see their life from a totally different perspective?

Discussion Starter Questions

- The first time you watched Pendulum Swings, what was your reaction to the director's (Dale) "And cut!"?
- Share a time you found yourself role-playing or acting like someone else in a real life situation.
- Sometimes we tend to look at others and compare, relate, or perceive their lives through our own interpretations. Is there a time you attended church and found yourself observing others thinking how different they are outside of church?
- Can you identify one more instance in your own life that would qualify as "playing church"?

It Was a Play?

Life Connection

My Life Connection *by Josh McDowell*

As an adult, my parents have revealed numerous childhood stories. In one of their memories, I dressed up in a three piece suit and tie. I line up all my stuffed animals on the floor in front of the sofa, on the sofa, and on the back of the sofa. My goal was to place the audience three rows deep before I would stand up on a chair and lead both singing and preaching to the attentive animals. I know it is true because my mother has pictures to prove it. Too bad the sound booth operator didn't know how to record back in those days, because those may have been some powerful sermons!

Playing make-believe is fine when you're five or six years old. And it wasn't so bad for me at twelve (I'm kidding I couldn't have been a day over eleven). But if we're still pretending every week at church there is something seriously wrong.

I served what you would call a good Bible believing, Bible teaching church for eight years and it wasn't until the last eighteen months or so that I realized that while I never really knew what I was doing. I was essentially playing "church." As I look back over those years I wonder how many American Christians basically "play church" even if they didn't know that is what they were doing. While serving that church I worked with children, directed outreach programs, managed the preschool and nursery volunteers, directed and trained Sunday School teachers, preached from time to time, and even lead a few mission trips. I loved that church. I loved the idea of that church. I loved the feeling of greatness that I felt being on staff at the biggest church in town. As the camera zoomed out, I began to see the same scene but from a different perspective. I realized that I was playing church and living primarily for my glory.

Both as a kid and as an adult, I remember checking my watch while sitting through a sermon to see how close it was until the congregation would sing "Just as I am" and we'd all be dismissed. I also can think of times when I sat and listened attentively as the speaker was sharing something relevant and valuable to my life.

It Was a Play?

I remember visiting kids on my Saturday morning bus route, the time with friends as we drove to the different homes, apartment complexes, and trailer parks was sometimes a lot of fun. Other times, when I made those visits alone, I was in a hurry to get it over with so I could move on to something else or something better that day.

I remember going door to door for outreach every Tuesday night and many times that experience was a ton of fun. We would laugh together as we drove to the designated neighborhood for canvassing that night, or we would laugh at each other as we became convinced that the address we were searching for couldn't possibly exist. But other times I remember thinking, I hope no one is at home because I'm ready to get back to the church, report "we were faithful, but no one was home", and go home.

Whether it was Sunday morning, Saturday bus outreach, or Tuesday night visitation there always came a time when the gospel was presented and someone was asked to make a decision for Christ. Then there would be a moment of prayer: "Dear Jesus, thank You for dying on the cross for my sins, please forgive me, I'm sorry for my sins and I want you in my life..." Now I'm not making conclusions about actual intentions of the heart or the prayers in those situations. But I do wonder if we play church more than we know. I'm not suggesting we stop Tuesday night outreach, bus ministry, or even the Sunday morning service, but I am encouraging us to stop pretending and share honestly what we are thinking.

You may be playing church if/when:

- You find yourself more occupied by the minutes of your watch ticking by rather than the sermon — you may be playing church.
- The results of your church responsibilities produce feelings of dread toward these responsibilities and/or a desire to step down from these responsibilities— you may be playing church.

- You fight with your family on Sunday morning as you are heading to church because your spouse isn't getting ready fast enough or the kids are arguing about what you laid out for them to wear — you might be playing church.
- You shake everyone's hand during the fellowship time but don't share a meal with anyone from the congregation during an average week — you might be playing church.
- Your brain immediately goes to judging someone at church because you can't believe their business practice and that they still come to church — you might be playing church.

We are all guilty of "playing church" from time to time, but what should we do about it?

If, for example, stepping down, no longer attending or giving up entirely is not the right answer, what *are* the answers?

As a small group, take a few moments to read through the scripture for today. Try and focus on reading these passages with an open mind, as if it were the first time you read this scripture. Ask and allow the Spirit of God to guide you and your conversation. See where listening to the Spirit of God and some simple discussion takes you. He may take you places you've never been before.

It Was a Play?

Relevant Scripture

As a small group, take a few moments to read through today's scripture, and focus on reading these passages without thinking you already know what they are saying. Ask and allow the Spirit of God to guide you and your conversation. See where listening to the Spirit of God and some simple discussion takes you.

Matthew 11:16-19

16 "But to what shall I compare this generation? It is like
children sitting in the market places, who call out to the other
children,
17 and say, 'We played the flute for you, and you did not dance;
we sang a dirge, and you did not mourn.'
18 "For John came neither eating nor drinking, and they say, 'He
has a demon!'
19 "The Son of Man came eating and drinking, and they say,
'Behold, a gluttonous man and a drunkard, a friend of tax
collectors and sinners!' Yet wisdom is vindicated by her deeds."

The discussion questions for today's small group study may help in understanding and discussing this passage of scripture, so if discussion doesn't begin after the reading of the scripture, continue to the discussion questions.

It Was a Play?

Discussion Questions

Matthew 11:16-19

16 "But to what shall I compare this generation? It
is like children sitting in the market places, who call out to
the other children, 17 and say, 'We played the flute for you, and
you did not dance; we sang a dirge, and you did
not mourn.' 18 "For John came neither eating nor drinking, and
they say, 'He has a demon!' 19 "The Son of Man came eating
and drinking, and they say, 'Behold, a gluttonous man and
a drunkard, a friend of tax collectors and sinners!' Yet wisdom
is vindicated by her deeds."

- This passage is speaking of children playing, maybe pretending to have a wedding party, and then getting bored and pretending to have a funeral. What did you and your friends play as children?

- Jesus was talking about the generation in which He was on earth, but do you see similarities with this generation?

- The people didn't appreciated John the Baptist and he *fit within their rules,* then they complained about *Jesus because He didn't fit* within their rules. Do you think we are a fickle society like that?

- Have you ever volunteered to do something at church just because you thought it was the right thing to do and not because you were passionate about it? Were you good at it or did you get burned out quickly?

- Have you ever quit something you were doing because no one appreciated your efforts?

- How could we quit playing church and start being the church?

It Was a Play?

- When you find yourself looking at your watch, or dreading a ministry you've signed up for, what are some ways you could stop pretending?

Take plenty of time in this discussion and allow each other to be honest. Think through and brainstorm ways to make your gatherings more effective.

CHAPTER 2

Doors and Hinges?

By Victor Gray

Movie Connection

Show movie clip #2 on Group DVD

Everyone has faced, at one time or another, a moral dilemma. There is some form of temptation, desire, thought, or a decision each of us have faced. We know what the right thing to do is, but we have an overwhelming desire to do the opposite. Those decisions are easy to make or easy to break; they are black and white, obvious, and clear-cut. In most cases, decisions may not be so clear. What we want to do isn't really wrong or sinful, it's just a bit misdirected. And rather than a bright blinking sign displaying which way we should go, there's only a still small voice in the back of our heads whispering, "This is a bad idea." We have a feeling in the pit of our stomach that what we want to do is *probably* the wrong thing, but the desire is so strong that the wrong thing doesn't seem so bad.

I think that Maria must have been struggling with that voice when her friends were on their way to party and she was by her car deciding if she would go home to be with her family or out "living it up" with the girls. The decision she made that seemed so inconsequential at the time would change the dynamic of her entire family. Sometimes big doors swing on small hinges, and the decisions we make today can affect a lifetime of tomorrows.

Discussion Starter Questions

- What do you think Maria was thinking in this scene?
- The dilemma of having fun verses what we should be doing starts at what age?
- If Maria's friends were not there to ask her to go out, do you think she would have went?

Doors and Hinges

Life Connection

My Life Connection *by Victor Gray*

Several years ago my sister was throwing a party for the praise band her son was a member of. The event was held at the Christian School he attended, and she asked me and my wife to come to the house and help chaperone. It was the first time I had the opportunity to meet many of my nephew's friends. They were a fantastic group of young people, each of them with a bright future ahead of them.

That night, as we sat around a bonfire, I began to talk with a girl my nephew had known for years (we'll call her Hanna). Hanna was an attractive girl with a bubbly personality and the voice of an angel. She showed her talent by singing praise songs around the fire while a few of her friends played acoustic six-string guitars.

"You should get one of these guys to go on the road with you, and you all could live off your music," I remember telling her. Hanna laughed. "Oh no," she replied. "My fiancé is a guitar player." I was shocked. I asked her if she was serious about being engaged. She assured me that she really was. "How old are you?" I asked her. "I'm 16. We're going to get married when I graduate next year."

I've never been one to keep my opinions to myself easily, and I decided that I wasn't about to start that night. "That's a really dumb idea," I told her quite matter-of-factly.

Hanna seemed to be equally shocked. "Why is that?" she asked, her voice full of outrage. "You're too young," I said. "I mean, do your parents know you're planning on getting married right after school?" "Oh sure, they're all for it." I was all the more stunned. "Well they're wrong too," I said.

The discussion went on for most of the remainder of the evening. I was convinced that a sixteen year old girl is not ready to make the decision of who she will spend the rest of her life with, and she was sure that she was in love and would be forever.

Remember, "Big doors, swing on little hinges" I thought to myself.

Just a couple of months ago, I was with my nephew and he was talking about a friend of his (we'll refer to as Macy) who was having a problem with her best friend. He wanted my opinion on what advice to offer her. He described that Macy felt like she was in the middle of her friend's marriage. Both of them were calling her cell phone several times a day, either to chat or to complain about the other. The wife in the relationship was going out with Macy almost every night, drinking, dancing, and flirting with guys all around town. She said that she felt like she'd married too early and never had a chance to be "young." There was only one part of the story that I didn't find shocking: The friend with the failing marriage was Hanna.

I wasn't the least bit happy that my reservations about the couple years before had been well-founded. It was sad. There's been many times in my own life when the wrong decision had lasting consequences. My advice to my nephew's friend Macy was to simply get out of the way! Only an act of God could keep Hanna's marriage from collapsing, and if Macy was still involved with the two of them, the rubble would fall on her.

In life, "big doors swing on little hinges." A little hinge in your life may be the decision to ignore advice, the little hinge may be the decision to flirt just a little bit as a married man or woman, or it could be something that seems much less significant. But every big path in your life will swing on a little decision here and there. How will Macy and Hanna's stories turn out? Only time will tell.

Doors and Hinges

Relevant Scripture

As a small group, take a few moments to read through today's scripture, and focus on reading these passages without thinking you already know what they are saying. Ask and allow the Spirit of God to guide you and your conversation. See where listening to the Spirit of God and some simple discussion takes you.

Jeremiah 29:11

11"For I know the plans that I have for you, declares the LORD, plans for welfare and not for calamity to give you a future and a hope."

How then can we discipline ourselves to make the right decision when the wrong decision is what we feel like we really want to do? I think we need to constantly question whether our decisions are wise. Are we choosing decisions that will give "a future and a hope?" Jesus Christ is the only perfect person in the history of the world. As cliché as it sounds, we should constantly ask ourselves, "What would Jesus do?"

In our marriages, what decisions will give our relationships "a future and a hope?" I honestly can't count the marriages that I've come to observe self-destruct for the very same things that went wrong between Dale and Maria. I've often heard married people talk about spending a great deal of time with friends of the opposite sex. They feel that it's their "right" to have these close relationships with their friends because "nothing's going on!"

What they fail to acknowledge is the emotional intimacy in and of itself wrong, an aspect of life that God wants us to enjoy with our spouse, not friends. So many times I've seen these types of friendships begin as two couples having a close friendship. There's nothing wrong with that, when the dynamic is as such that the wives are close with one another and the husbands are close with one another. When the husband of one couple and the wife of the other begin texting, calling, shopping, or having recreation with one another, they are setting their marriages up for a long hard fall. So often, I've watched emotional intimacy lead to physical intimacy, and two entire families end up paying the price for a friendship that initially said "nothing's going on."

Marriages aren't the only big doors that swing on little hinges. Finances can be destroyed with one small purchase paced on a credit card that leads to another, and another, and another. Every drug addict and alcoholic got their start with the first line, joint, or shot. Every venereal disease and pregnancy out of wed-lock began with a first kiss. Many decisions that we feel are inconsequential can have an enormous impact on our lives.

The discussion questions for today's small group study may help in understanding and discussing this passage of scripture. If discussion doesn't begin after the reading of the scripture, continue to the discussion questions.

Discussion Questions

- What do you think God's best "hope and future" is for your finances?

- What do you think God's best "hope and future" is for your health?

- What do you think God's best "hope and future" is for you when it comes to your physical or sexual life?

Take plenty of time in this discussion and allow each other to be honest. Think through and brainstorm ways to make your gatherings more effective.

CHAPTER 3

Liar, Liar, Pants on Fire?

By Bob Templeton

3. Liar, Liar, Pants on Fire

Movie Connection

Show movie clips #3 on Group DVD

In the beginning scene of the movie Dale and his daughters, Jenna and Jessica, are going to the concert. When Jenna asks where her mother is, Dale tells Jenna that she is probably stuck in traffic. Dale knows where his wife is, but he is trying to protect the girls by lying about their mother's whereabouts. Dale makes a judgment call and decides that lying here is better than telling the truth.

Discussion Starter Questions

- How often do we do the same thing, thinking that we are protecting someone we love by lying to them?
- Where do we draw the line between truth and protection?
- Is there really such a thing as a "white" lie?
- Does God look at the motive behind the lie or just see the lie as sin?

These are some tough questions but they confront us almost daily as we live in this fallen world.

Liar, Liar, Pants on Fire

Life Connection

My Life Connection *by Bob Templeton*

There have been many movies dealing with the effects of lying or not lying. In *Pinocchio* a wooden puppet's nose grew every time he lied. It would be interesting, just for a day, to see how long our noses grew through the little lies we tell. In *Liar Liar* a lawyer, played by Jim Carrey, is the victim of his son's birthday wish and is not able to tell a lie for 24 hours. The comedy that ensues is about blunt opinions of telling people what he really thinks rather than lying. The issue here is that our opinions are not always the truth, they are just our opinions. Truth is more than not telling a lie. Truth is not *error* and must be logically and factually correct. Truth is not deception. Some believe that truth is relevant (different for different people). If that were true, then it would not fit the definition of being logically and factually correct. In other words, truth does not contradict itself. If truth is relevant, then by its very nature, two people's truth can contradict each other. Some call this the law of non-contradiction. Pretty deep stuff, huh?

The bottom line is, there must be a standard or basis for truth outside of individual human philosophy. For a Christian that standard is God and His Word. Jesus said, "He was the Way, the Truth, and the Life." God came to earth and presented to man a man like God meant him to be. That man was Jesus Christ and his life displayed moment by moment the truth of God. Jesus didn't just live in a vacuum; He lived for thirty-three years on earth just like you and me. He had conversations, worked, ate meals, and did life with others. He was tempted in all points such as we are; therefore it stands to reason that He was tempted to lie. Yet he lived this life, without sin, and left us an example of a man filled with all of God. The source that powered His life was God, and today as believers we have that same power in the person of the Holy Spirit living inside us.

One thing we know about the life of Christ was that He spoke the truth. Many times it was not very popular to do so, but He did it anyway. He revealed people's real motives and the anger He stirred up in the religious leaders of His day eventually led Him to the cross. The question before us remains, "How do we not lie and yet still protect our loved ones?" As we look at Christ's example two things should assist us in this matter. First, when confronted with a question that could cause controversy, Jesus answered the question with another question. He did this both to reveal motives and to cause the listeners to think. Secondly, Jesus, filled with the Spirit of God, many times said nothing. It is our nature to open our mouth in situations, even without anything valuable to say. We are not disciplined to season our words before speaking.

Parenting is a difficult journey. Chances are we are going to make mistakes along the way, but we are promised by Scripture that God will give us all we need when we need it. The question of physical safety being compromised by lying is often discussed as a justification of lying. The biblical illustration of Rahab lying about the spies becomes the proof text for most of these discussions. I am convinced that God hates lying and that lying is a sin. We can sit around and make up what-if scenarios all day long but in the trenches, decisions must be made and action must be taken. I only trust that as we are placed in difficult positions that we make sure we are filled with the Holy Spirit and that he is directing the words we speak and the actions we take.

Liar, Liar, Pants on Fire

Relevant Scripture

As a small group, take a few moments to read through today's scripture, and focus on reading these passages without thinking you already know what they are saying. Ask and allow the Spirit of God to guide you and your conversation. See where listening to the Spirit of God and some simple discussion takes you.

John 14:6

Jesus said to him, "I am the way, and the truth, and the life; no one comes to the Father but through Me.

Colossians 2:8

See to it that no one takes you captive through philosophy and empty deception, according to the tradition of men, according to the elementary principles of the world, rather than according to Christ.

Hebrews 4:15

For we do not have a high priest who cannot sympathize with our weaknesses, but One who has been tempted in all things as we are, yet without sin.

Psalms 120:2

Deliver my soul, O LORD, from lying lips, from a deceitful tongue.

Proverbs 6:16-18

16 There are six things which the LORD hates, yes, seven which
are an abomination to Him:
17 Haughty eyes, a lying tongue, And hands that shed innocent
blood,
18 A heart that devises wicked plans,
Feet that run rapidly to evil,

Liar, Liar, Pants on Fire

John 8:43-45

43 Why do you not understand what I am saying? It is because
you cannot hear My word.
44You are of your father the devil, and you want to do the desires
of your father He was a murderer from the beginning, and does
not stand in the truth because there is no truth in him whenever
he speaks a lie, he speaks from his own nature, for he is a liar and
the father of lies.
45But because I speak the truth, you do not believe Me.

The discussion questions for today's small group study may help in understanding and discussing this passage of scripture. If discussion doesn't begin after the reading of the scripture, continue to the discussion questions.

Discussion Questions

- Why do we tell "white" lies?
- If you were Dale, how would you have answered Jenna?
- What is our greatest need when living out our lives in a Christ-like manner?
- Is it ever right to do something wrong?

Bonus:

- Can you give the group a personal example of a time when you were tempted to lie but didn't, or when you did lie and the outcomes that followed?
- How do we justify deception and lying in our minds?
- How is an opinion different from truth?

Take plenty of time in this discussion and allow each other to be honest. Think through and brainstorm ways to make your gatherings more effective.

CHAPTER 4

Losing Something Precious?

By Bill Carrier

Movie Connection

Show movie clip #4 on Group DVD

In the beginning of the movie there is a scene where Dale briefly loses sight of his youngest daughter, Jessica. The panic of every parent comes to life as this father desperately seeks to find his daughter, while the thoughts of abduction are racing through his mind. Fortunately, he finds his daughter and the situation is resolved without any incident. He later promises his daughter that he will never leave her alone again and will always come to find her. Not all stories turn out this way and some parents do go through the agony of child abduction.

Later in the movie, when it is evident that divorce may be unavoidable, Dale has a conversation with his daughter, Jenna. He warns her of the possible marital separation and the inevitable attacks that will be made on his character. He lets her know how he feels, and no matter what she hears from others, he loves her and will always love her. Finally, he does lose them and becomes the "part-time parent", which is something he never wanted to be. At that point his world has crashed around him as everything he holds dear has been stripped from his grasp. There also comes a point where Dale is faced with the decision to live up to his promise and be there for his children. In a dream, he is reminded by the presence of his father to stand up and be the dad he is meant to be. This event becomes a turning point in Dale's life.

Losing Something Precious

Discussion Starter Questions

- How did you feel when Dale was panicking?
- Have you ever found yourself frantically searching for something important?
- Have you ever seen a loss coming ahead of time and tried to prepare for it?

Life Connection

My Life Connection *by Bill Carrier*

Unfortunately, real loss happens every day. This has happened and will continue to happen until the end of time. I am sure we all can identify with this situation and we could name the people in our network of friends that have been touched by such a tragedy of the family. We may also know the pain of losing love ones through death or broken fellowship because of strife and tension in the family. In short, the separation that comes in families can happen suddenly and without much warning. We are met with the choice of throwing in the towel or standing up to the adversity and becoming better, stronger individuals.

We really don't need someone else's story to help us think about loss, because the loss that we remember is more real to us than any loss we've can hear about. Take some time together and share about how you felt when you were faced with loss or the possibility of loss.

Relevant Scripture

As a small group, take a few moments to read through today's scripture, and focus on reading these passages without thinking you already know what they are saying. Ask and allow the Spirit of God to guide you and your conversation. See where listening to the Spirit of God and some simple discussion takes you.

In times like these we can question why God may have let something undesirable to happen, feeling as though we are being punished, or worse, that God is playing some silly game for His amusement. While God may be using situations of life to move and mold us, the fact of His love for us should never be in question.

Even when Dale was in the depths of his pain, the way God felt about him never varied. We too can know that our Father, as Dale told his daughter, will never stop loving us and will never change His mind about us. We may never get a full explanation about why we go through circumstances but we can always count on the stability of the Father's love. Just like Jenna could not understand, due to her limited knowledge, we also struggle to see the relevance of God's actions in our lives. But Jenna trusted the words of her father and kept them close to her heart. We also need to remember and remind ourselves of the love our Father has for us and the great lengths He went to secure us to Himself. The Father had lost something precious to Him in the Garden of Eden and Jesus won us back on the cross through His shed blood. We might not fully understand the method He chose but we can appreciate the motivation of His love.

The very thing Dale feared the most did happen, and he did suffer some horrible pain in the process; however, God showed Himself faithful by bringing Dale back from the brink of self-destruction. Sometimes the very thing we fear the most is the very thing God wants to use to grow us and change us into the image of His Son. Dale's daughters were precious to him before the pain and agony of the divorce and became even more precious to him after the divorce. The trails of life have an incredible effect on us and can leave lasting scars and wounds that never seem to fully heal. These are the moments God is using to make us realize what is precious and what is trivial. He uses the fires of life to burn away anything that doesn't look like Christ. He also uses these times to help us fully understand His love toward us and give us more knowledge about Him.

Romans 7:38-39 Describe what you hear God telling you.

I John 3:1-2 Describe how this makes you feel.

Additional scriptures

Psalm 22:24

Romans 5:8

Romans 8:18

Philippians 3:10

The discussion questions for today's small group study may help in understanding and discussing this passage of scripture. If discussion doesn't begin after the reading of the scripture, continue to the discussion questions.

Discussion Questions

- What is the thing/person you fear to lose most?
- How would that loss change your life?
- Would the loss change your opinion about God?
- Does God play games with people's lives? Explain your answer.
- What have you lost in the past that affected your relationship with God for positive or negative?

Take plenty of time in this discussion and allow each other to be honest. Think through and brainstorm ways to make your gatherings more effective

CHAPTER 5

Church: The Team Sport

By Bill Carrier

Movie Connection

Show movie clip #5 on Group DVD

In the movie there is a scene where Dale and the girls are going to church and his wife, Maria, is staying home because she is hung over. The older daughter, Jenna, does not understand the reason behind her mother's lack of interest, but she did know that the real truth was not being told. We are not trying to make drinking alcohol the focal point of this discussion because there are other excuses people use for not attending church. The point is that Maria is having subtle pressure put on her to be a part of the family, and in her mind she must choose between what she wants to do versus being a "good person." This contributes to the increasing distance within the relationship and does nothing to support the chances of bringing them together.

Discussion Starter Questions

- Have you even been the one who did not want to attend church?
- What if you can't decide on which church to attend as a family?
- What are some things that you could do if your spouse does not want to attend church because the social scene is getting in the way?

Life Connection

My Life Connection *by Bill Carrier*

We are encouraged to be involved in each believer's life in more ways than just church attendance. Church attendance may be a part of the Christian life but it does not make one good or bad. Only the life of the Father lived out through His children is effective in changing lives. In the movie, Dale wanted to have his wife as a part of the family's activities in church, but he isolated her due to her lack of desire to go. Pressure to perform where there is no desire breeds contempt.

Many Christians today are leaving what we would call the "traditional model of the American church" for more unconventional methods of assembling with believers. This has also divided families because sometimes one spouse wants to be a part of a fellowship that is familiar to their upbringing while the other spouse wants to break out of the traditional mold to seek something that is more personal. This is the point where the "Biblical" arguments begin and hearing ends. We tend to want to either force believers into or out of the traditional model. The truth is that both sides are wrong. The answer to the problem is freedom, freedom to go and freedom to stay. The Father wants to have a relationship with us and not our methods. He wants to be a part of the communion with the church, not the style of the church. Around the world every culture has its own unique style and traditions that are not found anywhere else. There are some commonalities but each culture brings a special flavor and diversity that needs no approval or disapproval from other cultures. One is not better that the other, just different. Our Father speaks every language and understands the heart of every believer.

So what is the answer? Who is right and who is wrong? The answer is freedom. The way the Father treats us is how we treat each other. Very little is given in the New Testament discussing the style of the church and a minimal amount addresses the structure of the church. The attitude of the church is much more important than the hard fast rules of the structure of the church. Humility, kindness, compassion, patience, and most of all love are more important than the style of the fellowship you attend. Jesus said it was by our love they will know we are His disciples, not our buildings, ministries, sermons, rules, studies, doctrine, bylaws or style. Love casts our doubt, fear and oppression. Forced performance is death not life, and forced performance can only produce death. God knew we could not perform so He sent Jesus to do it for us. If God knows it is impossible for us to perform to perfection then why are we trying to burden each other with performance demands?

Relevant Scripture

As a small group, take a few moments to read through today's scripture, and focus on reading these passages without thinking you already know what they are saying. Ask and allow the Spirit of God to guide you and your conversation. See where listening to the Spirit of God and some simple discussion takes you.

1 Corinthians 7:12-13

12 But to the rest I say, not the Lord, that if any brother has a
wife who is an unbeliever, and she consents to live with him, he
must not divorce her.
13 And a woman who has an unbelieving husband, and he
consents to live with her, she must not send her husband away.

This scenario is as old as the idea of coming together to be with a fellowship of believers. The Apostle Paul addresses the idea of conflict in the home concerning Christianity. The instruction Paul gives is to leave them alone and let them choose the direction they wish to take.

One of the hardest things for a human being to do is let someone be free to choose. We try to force, badger, plead, beg, browbeat, guilt, coerce, and shame people to believe and behave in the way that seems right to us. We may be right in theory, but our tactic is wrong. A relationship with God and believers are decisions made by the individual, not by the group.

The more things change, the more they stay the same. Many homes are in conflict because one spouse is trying, for their own good, to force the other to either come to church or make them profess a belief in Christ when they have no desire to do so. The New Testament Christian's proper reaction to this situation is to leave it in the hands of the Holy Spirit. By the believer's actions the love of God and the message of the gospel is proclaimed. This is how the Father approaches humanity, with demonstrations of love and messages of freedom from death, sin, and eternal separation. Jesus proclaimed the love of the Father by coming to us, not by us going to Him.

The discussion questions for today's small group study may help in understanding and discussing this passage of scripture. If discussion doesn't begin after the reading of the scripture, continue to the discussion questions.

Discussion Questions

- What are some of the traditions you hold closest?
- Is there a biblical basis for these traditions? If so, where is it found?
- Read Hebrews 10:19-25 and discuss the context of verse 25.
- Read Philippians 2:1-8 and describe the attitude of believers.
- How close is the modern church to what is described in scriptures?
- How do we help families that are like Dale and Maria?
- What do we have to be to let others be free?

Take plenty of time in this discussion and allow each other to be honest. Think through and brainstorm ways to make your gatherings more effective.

CHAPTER 6

Better a Witness in the Bar, or Outside

By Mary Reid

Better Witness in the Bar, or Outside?

Movie Connection

Show movie clip #6 on Group DVD

Poor Dale: Desperately wanting to make his marriage work, he finds himself in the bar. Completely uneasy and far away from his comfort zone, he ends up spending the night alone watching his wife fit in perfectly. How awkward he must have felt being there watching Maria, his wife, dance the night away.

Discussion Starter Questions

- What could have been Dale's real reasons for going to the club with Maria and her friends?
- When accused of not liking Maria's friends, why does Dale lash out? Was Dale's response justifiable or lacking the characteristics of a good witness?

Life Connection

My Life Connection *by Mary Reid*

Witnessing to someone is much deeper than expressing a few words to a complete stranger. The heart of it is when we share our lives with people and build real relationships. To try and witness to people in either situation, without forming genuine relationships, first becomes second rate to building real relationships.

A lot of times when we approach witnessing, we end up treating everyone the same. We say the same things over and over until it becomes thoughtless and emotionless. Our religious efforts to coax someone into going to our place of worship will not cause them to become curious about the God we serve but rather the expression of God's love in our lives will captivate someone, and that can only be seen in everyday life.

Jesus spent a lot of time in places that the religious people of his day didn't agree with. He spent his days building relationships with sinners, tax collectors, and even prostitutes. These were the people that religion thought to be unworthy. I don't think Jesus just went and knocked on their doors and handed out scrolls to invite them to the local synagogue. He built relationships and shared experiences with genuine fondness for people. He didn't treat them the way that the religious people treated them. He loved them and accepted them. He didn't run out of their presence fearful that someone would see him in a place like that. He didn't turn his back on them because they didn't fit into the box of religion. He loved them where and as they were.

Sometimes we get so wrapped up in behaving properly that we don't seem genuine to people. Having flaws doesn't make us bad Christians; it just makes us human and possibly more approachable. Not to say that we should behave badly to make ourselves more approachable, but perhaps we should spend less time trying to hide the flaws we have and more time being real with the people God has placed in our lives. If someone cannot walk with me where I am going they probably cannot relate to me very well. We have been taught that we shouldn't go to certain places because it will make us look like the world, but how do you share the gospel with the world without going into the world? Just like going to church can't make you a Christian, going to the bar can't make you "un-Christian."

Relevant Scripture

As a small group, take a few moments to read through today's scripture, and focus on reading these passages without thinking you already know what they are saying. Ask and allow the Spirit of God to guide you and your conversation. See where listening to the Spirit of God and some simple discussion takes you.

Matthew 9:10-13

10 Then it happened that as Jesus was reclining at the table in the house, behold, many tax collectors and sinners came and were dining with Jesus and His disciples.
11 When the Pharisees saw this, they said to His disciples, "Why is your Teacher eating with the tax collectors and sinners ?"
12 But when Jesus heard this, He said, "It is not those who are healthy who need a physician, but those who are sick.
13 "But go and learn what this means: 'I DESIRE COMPASSION, AND NOT SACRIFICE,' for I did not come to call the righteous, but sinners."

John 12:1-3

1 Jesus, therefore, six days before the Passover, came to Bethany where Lazarus was, whom Jesus had raised from the dead.
2 So they made Him a supper there, and Martha was serving ; but Lazarus was one of those reclining at the table with Him.
3 Mary then took a pound of very costly perfume of pure nard, and anointed the feet of Jesus and wiped His feet with her hair ; and the house was filled with the fragrance of the perfume.

Luke 10:38-42

38 Now as they were traveling along, He entered a village ; and a woman named Martha welcomed Him into her home.

39 She had a sister called Mary, who was seated at the Lord's
feet, listening to His word.
40 But Martha was distracted with all her preparations ; and she
came up to Him and said, "Lord, do You not care that my sister
has left me to do all the serving alone ? Then tell her to help me."
41 But the Lord answered and said to her, "Martha, Martha, you
are worried and bothered about so many things ;
42 but only one thing is necessary, for Mary has chosen the good
part, which shall not be taken away from her."

The discussion questions for today's small group study may help in understanding and discussing this passage of scripture. If discussion doesn't begin after the reading of the scripture, continue to the discussion questions.

Discussion Questions

- Placed in a similar environment would you be like Dale, completely uncomfortable, or like Maria, dancing the night away?
- Do you think that it is wrong for us, as Christians, to even walk into a bar?
- We've all seen street preachers; do you think that someone trying to witness would be more effective preaching outside the bar? Why or why not?
- Do you think your presence in a bar would damage your witness with someone? Why or why not?

Take plenty of time in this discussion and allow each other to be honest. Think through and brainstorm ways to make your gatherings more effective.

CHAPTER 7

When Temptation is Wearing a Short, Tight Skirt

By Paul Withrow

Movie Connection

Show movie clip #7 on Group DVD

Stephanie approaches Dale at the commercial shoot and offers him her phone number, along with an invitation. Dale seems surprised and really doesn't know what to say, so he says nothing. He just watches her walk away. After thinking about what just happened, Dale throws away the phone number, ending the temptation. He does take one last look at the garbage can before he leaves to go home.

Think about the "mental ping pong" most people would have in their head. The decision had probably already been made about a situation like this long before Dale had the temptation in his hands.

Discussion Starter Questions

- For most married men would this be a normal occurrence?
- Could it be that spiritual forces are at work behind the scenes?
- Would these dark forces be aware of Dale's marriage problems?
- Considering that our battles are not against flesh and blood, what could possibly be the motive of the temptress, Stephanie?

- Situations that Christians often refer to as "temptation to sin" are seen simply as "opportunities for fun" to many others. Christians deny themselves where others indulge themselves. Is this a good practice?

Life Connection

My Life Connection *by Paul Withrow*

Some of us can look back and remember trying to live out the rules and morals that we were taught at home. In the meantime, we were also watching those around us "enjoying" themselves. Sinful activity does have pleasure for a season. Many in the world have given up the struggle against bad behavior. As the old saying goes, if it feels good do it. Yet, Christians desire to walk the walk, not just talk the talk. The problem is that the same discouragement occurs. Temptations do present a battle. What power do we have to defeat such an enemy? If Christians are employing the same tools then we are going to meet with the same exhaustion and ultimately the same defeat. If the world cannot win by wanting morality and employing will power, why is the church trying the same?

Spiritual Battles require spiritual weapons.

Reading the law and attempting to obey it is very frustrating. The problem with this is that it's devoid of any relationship with Jesus or His Spirit. Desiring to be moral isn't enough to keep us. The temptation of pleasure is too strong. When Jesus saves us, we begin to conflict with our own moral failures. The idea of just being moral for morality sake is no longer part of the equation. Because our desire is to please the Lord we are open to His teachings and His motivations through the Holy Spirit. We begin to desire what He desires. What a contrast!

Before, we were trying to be moral through our will power; afterward, we realize that all the power of heaven is at our fingertips. We can walk in the Spirit and, in doing so, we will not be carrying out the desires of the flesh. Walking is a positive direction of obedience with momentum toward doing the will of God, as opposed to waiting on temptations to come and then making an attempt to defeat it by your own will power.

Therefore, morality for morality sake is a dead-end road. The result will be self-righteousness. Obeying a law for the sake of obeying a law outside of a relationship with Jesus is legalism.

Legalism produces a stiff neck along with pride. Following closely is a judgmental attitude toward others: No love, no fulfillment, no joy.

When Dale is faced with the temptation to be unfaithful to Maria, we see he didn't give in. Beneath the surface is the real question: Why? Was he really motivated by love, love for Maria, love for his daughters, love for God and his Christian brothers and sisters, or love even for Stephanie? Or did he say no because it was the right thing to do?

Relevant Scripture

As a small group, take a few moments to read through today's scripture, and focus on reading these passages without thinking you already know what they are saying. Ask and allow the Spirit of God to guide you and your conversation. See where listening to the Spirit of God and some simple discussion takes you.

Gal. 5:16

But I say, walk by the Spirit, and you will not carry out the desire of the flesh.

I John 2:15-17

15 Do not love the world nor the things in the world. If anyone loves the world, the love of the Father is not in him.
16 For all that is in the world, the lust of the flesh and the lust of the eyes and the boastful pride of life, is not from the Father, but is from the world.
17 The world is passing away, and also its lusts; but the one who does the will of God lives forever.

John3:16

16 "For God so loved the world, that He gave His only begotten Son, that whoever believes in Him shall not perish, but have eternal life.

I John3:16

16 This is how we know what love is: Jesus Christ laid down his life for us. And we ought to lay down our lives for our brothers.

The discussion questions for today's small group study may help in understanding and discussing this passage of scripture. If discussion doesn't begin after the reading of the scripture, continue to the discussion questions.

Discussion Questions

- How does a happy marriage help men in facing temptations like this?
- Would a stressful, struggling marriage make temptation more difficult?
- How could we prepare for the temptations that will arise in our life?
- What is your role as a spouse in preparation for your partner's future temptation?
- How do we teach these ideas and principles to our children?
- Let's discuss the difference between walking in the Spirit and battling temptation through will power?
- How do we walk in the Spirit?

Take plenty of time in this discussion and allow each other to be honest. Think through and brainstorm ways to make your gatherings more effective.

CHAPTER 8

Family, Friends and Other Negative Influences

By Jennifer Rahn

Movie Connection

Show movie clip #8 on Group DVD

In the movie, there is a scene where Jenna is huddled in the corner while her mother, grandmother, and friend are in the kitchen laughing and mocking Dale. My father was obviously not there for this moment, but from the way I described it to him he somehow composed an almost exact replica in the movie itself. I have not revisited this moment much since it happened. It took me more than a few times to make it through this scene in the movie as my eyes would fill with tears to the point of blurring the screen. This scene was monumental for me. In real life, this moment was the point when I had taken in too much of the mind games, and I was breaking. I was tired of being strong. I just wanted to be a "normal" pre-adolescent child and have my happy family back.

Discussion Starter Questions

- It is important to remember how our actions are *permanent*. Can you name a time when you felt betrayed by someone close to you? How did you react? Is there anything you would change about your reaction?

- I may never understand how or why family members choose to hurt others close to them. It seems they are blinded by how hurtful their words and actions are, or how their present actions will have future consequences. How do you relate to the storyline described on the previous page? What do you know about unforeseen consequences?
- What are examples of "actions speak louder than words" in your own life? Do you know anyone who has influenced you or modeled this concept to you?

Life Connection

My Life Connection *by Jennifer Rahn*

I distinctly recall the emotions that followed as my father's words reached out to me: "I will never lie to you, and I will always love you." These words were vital as he had just revealed to me that people around me may, directly or indirectly, speak negatively about him, about our family, and about our situation which they were uninformed about. This concept was overwhelmingly confusing. Why would anyone speak against my father in such a way? At the time, I could not fathom the reality headed my way.

I remember the first time I was approached at school. It was lunch time, and I was waiting my turn to pay at the end of the cafeteria lunch line. My friend's mother, who volunteered at the school, made a snide remark to me about my father's character and how I was being swayed wrongfully to take his side. I was so embarrassed that I honestly don't even remember what the exact comments from her were. I paused and stared at her while holding my lunch tray, and without a word spoken in return I walked away. This was the first moment in which I replayed the words my father said to me. Tears repressed, I smiled and sat down with my friends to have lunch.

It grew worse. Every time I was invited over to play and hang out with my friends, their mothers would confront me, pull me aside, and ramble a number of hurtful things regarding my father (and sometimes towards me as well). My teachers would ask me to stay after class to "check in on me" (however, it was merely an excuse for them to intervene with their ill-informed opinions). Each time these events occurred, I would listen in my mind for my father's comforting words.

I can't begin to express how difficult it was to have my entire world crash behind the scenes while I did my best to remain composed and strong on the outside. School was supposed to be a safe place for me. It was a place away from those who were hurting me. All of the sudden it seemed like there was nowhere safe, and I had to be on guard constantly.

Invaluable life skills and learning can come from any situation, including those deemed painful and inextricably wrong. I witnessed first-hand a father who didn't have to prove himself in the midst of adversary because he had already been living genuine and dedicated to our family the entire time. The foundation he built with my sister and I was so strong that even an army of destructive lies could not make me question who he was. During these initial years, I had lost all stability and the ability to freely give my trust to others. The only constant thing I knew was my father. Those who *live* their lives daily as the person they say they are do not (later) have to prove themselves to *tell* people who they think they are. It is the most bold and empowering example of the phrase "actions speak louder than words". Words can be a quick fix or cover up, but actions are a foundation as a result to time.

Relevant Scripture

As a small group take a few moments to read through the scripture for today and attempt to read these passages without thinking you already know what these passages are saying. Ask and allow the Spirit of God to guide you and your conversation. See where listening to the Spirit of God and some simple discussion takes you.

The scriptures not only instruct us regarding what to do when someone strays, but also tells us how to do so. Consider the following verses as you think about Dale's phone conversation with Jake as well as your own life experiences.

James 1:19 (NIV)

19 My dear brothers and sisters, take note of this: Everyone should be quick to listen, slow to speak and slow to become angry

Ephesians 4:25 (NIV)

25 Therefore each of you must put off falsehood and speak truthfully to your neighbor, for we are all members of one body

I Timothy 4: 11-12 (NIV)

11 Command and teach these things
12 Don't let anyone look down on your because you are young, but set an example for the believers in speech, in conduct, in love, in faith, and in purity

Matthew 6: 15 (NIV)

15 But if you do not forgive others their sins, your Father will not forgive your sins

Ephesians 4:32 (NIV)

32 Be kind and compassionate to one another, forgiving each other, just as in Christ God forgave you

Luke 6:37 (NIV)

37 Do not judge, and you will not be judged. Do not condemn, and
you will not be condemned. Forgive, and you will be forgiven

The discussion questions for today's small group study may help in understanding and discussing this passage of scripture, so if discussion doesn't begin after the reading of the scripture, continue to the discussion questions.

Discussion Questions

- It is hard to hear people or experience those who speak negatively of others or our self. Ultimately, it provides no person gain and instead damages another human being. How do you think you would have reacted to Jenna's mother if you were her son/daughter? What if you were her husband, friend, family member?

- As children, we are sometimes not given the opportunity to be heard. How does this affect the way we listen and value our children's (or children you know) words and expression of feelings?

- We have all been guilty of hurting others, whether by words or actions, intentionality or unintentionally. Have you been in a situation where you were hurt, betrayed, deceived so badly that it was hard to forgive that person? Have you forgiven them? What did you do, or could you do, to truly forgive those who have hurt you?

Take plenty of time in this discussion and allow each other to be honest. Think through and brainstorm ways to make your gatherings more effective.

CHAPTER 9

Friends That Kick You While You're Down

By Robbie Starnes

Movie Connection

Show movie clip #9 on Group DVD

Like a verbal machine gun, Jake begins to fire his chastising bullets at Dale. Interestingly, Jake has had no association with Dale in a long time. Jake's concern for Dale is void of Christian compassion and understanding. Jake's critical comments and his attempts to hold Dale accountable fall on deaf ears. Any opportunity to lovingly focus Dale's attention on his real need of restored fellowship with God was lost.

Discussion Starter Questions

- When other Christians fail to sympathize with your struggles and circumstances, how does that make you feel?

- When you've responded critically or judgmentally toward others (in their struggle / circumstances) how did they respond? Think of a specific instance you can share regarding what your wrong response looked like?

- When bad turns to worse for someone in your life, how can initially with-holding judgmental responses eventually open the door to an opportunity to provide loving accountability and correction? Can you think of an example in your own life?

Life Connection

My Life Connection *by Robbie Starnes*

As a young believer, I was critical of others who seemed to be more tolerant about the sin they allowed in their lives. I didn't know how to love them. I even questioned their salvation because of what I saw as a "casual approach" to obvious sinful practices.

My strong focus on "truth" left little room for "grace." Looking back, I realize that truth must be tempered with grace, and that "grace" must be balanced with "truth." Truth without grace looks like Christian legalism, while grace without truth appears to be Christian Hedonism. Hedonism is a school of thought which argues that pleasure is the only intrinsic good. This is often used as a justification for evaluating actions in terms of how much pleasure and how little pain (i.e. suffering) they produce. In very simple terms, a hedonist strives to maximize this net pleasure (pleasure minus pain).

I didn't realize at the time that I was on the legalistic side of the pendulum's swing. I justified my thinking from a serious approach to God's holiness. My pride was eventually swallowed up by my personal failure to live up to my own expectations. Enter mercy and grace.

One snapshot of my journey toward mercy and grace happened in the Navy. I joined the Navy after high school. I wanted to serve the Lord and I was fervent about studying the scriptures and sharing my faith. I made lots of friends, but it was difficult to find others to fellowship with. There weren't many Christians on the ship, which I knew of, but there were plenty of mockers and tempters. "Hey, come on, just one drink" or "Hey look at that girl's butt," (but they didn't say butt) were common teasers. I didn't want to give a "holier than thou" impression, but it did give me an opportunity to be real with them about my walk with the Lord. They didn't seem to care, but I can't help to think that in their heart of hearts, they really wanted life change. I continued to buddy with them, however; limiting where I went and what I did.

Unfortunately, by the end of my enlistment, I weakened and started partying with them. Instead of leading them to the Lord, I followed them to the bar. Sin breeds sin, and before long, by my lifestyle you would not have known that I was a Christian. My testimony shipwrecked. It all seemed like a bad dream. I was doing the same things and worse things than I had criticized other Christians for. My "all or nothing" approach to the Christian life revealed itself on the hedonistic side of the pendulum swing. As a result, I understood God's grace in a whole new light.

As a result of my own failures and God's unconditional love, I am learning to love others where they are. His holiness is the reality of who I am in Christ. His grace is the practical medium that allows me to live it out.

Relevant Scripture

As a small group, take a few moments to read through today's scripture, and focus on reading these passages without thinking you already know what they are saying. Ask and allow the Spirit of God to guide you and your conversation. See where listening to the Spirit of God and some simple discussion takes you.

The scriptures not only instruct us regarding what to do when someone strays, but it also tells us how to do so. Consider the following verses as you think about Dale's phone conversation with Jake as well as your own life experiences.

James 5:19-20

19 My brethren, if any among you strays from the truth and one turns him back,
20 let him know that he who turns a sinner from the error of his way will save his soul from death.

I Peter 4:8

Above all, keep fervent in your love for one another, because love covers a multitude of sins.

Galatians 6:1

Brethren, even if anyone is caught in any trespass, you who are spiritual, restore such a one in a spirit of gentleness; each one looking to yourself, so that you too will not be tempted.

II Corinthians 2:6-8

6 Sufficient for such a one is this punishment which was inflicted by the majority,
7 so that on the contrary you should rather forgive and comfort him, otherwise such a one might be overwhelmed by excessive sorrow.
8 Wherefore I urge you to reaffirm your love for him.

For further study, consider:

II Thessalonians 3:14, 15

II Kings 12:1-7

The discussion questions for today's small group study may help in understanding and discussing this passage of scripture. If discussion doesn't begin after the reading of the scripture, continue to the discussion questions.

Discussion Questions

- How would, "Let the one without sin cast the first stone," apply to the way we handle sensitive situations involving sinful behavior?

- Why is it so difficult to associate with other Christians/friends who have strayed into an immoral lifestyle of drugs, alcohol addiction, sexual sin, child abuse, etc?

- How much of the difficulty involves your fear of what others will think of you if you love and support the person who has been caught in sin?

- Think of someone you know who is astray. How can you, "in a spirit of gentleness", practically show them that you love them right where they are?

- How can we come alongside those who are living in obvious disobedience without enabling or condoning their behavior?

- Talk about personal experiences. Have you ever been hit by the VMG, Verbal Machine Gun?

Take plenty of time in this discussion and allow each other to be honest. Think through and brainstorm ways to make your gatherings more effective.

CHAPTER 10

Guilt

By John Keogh

Movie Connection

Show movie clip #10 on Group DVD

Dale sits alone on the couch in the trailer he's just thrashed. He's cradling a picture frame in his hands, a photograph of his daughters, Jenna and Jessica. The girls are smiling big and sweet beneath the cracked glass.

Dale breaks down. From inside his jacket, he pulls out a gun. "I'm sorry," he sobs. "I'm sorry."

On the night she got lost at the concert, Dale promised Jessica that he'd never lose her again. It's a promise he hasn't been able to keep.

His marriage is over, his children have seen their family torn apart, and only see their father when the courts allow. Dale can't provide for them because despair and addiction have got a hold of him, and he's lost his work and the will to get back on his feet.

His daughters have seen him dragged from their house in handcuffs like a criminal. And now, because Dale failed to keep his word, the girls are grieving the death of a friend. Dale is crushed. The guilt of it all is too much.

To some extent, most of us have been in Dale's shoes. We may never have experienced the same things, found ourselves at the very end of our rope, or driven to suicidal despair; however, we know what it is like to be troubled by guilt. The type of guilt can be one of past mistakes, bad decisions, broken relationships, personal failures, or even hurting others. We are haunted sometimes by memories of sinful living that flood us with guilt and shame.

Sadly, many of us carry this guilt around with us every day. Perhaps, without fully realizing it, this affects our everyday lives. And as Christians, guilt can be a major hindrance to our walk with God.

Take some time to discuss the following questions, with openness and honesty.

Discussion Starter Questions

- Have you ever found yourself in Dale's position: beaten down by guilt and failure and seeing no way out?
- In what ways does guilt affect our everyday lives and our walk with God?
- Why do you think we allow guilt to have such a strong hold over us?
- What would you say to a friend or fellow Christian struggling with guilt?

Life Connection

My Life Connection *by John Keogh*

In the summer of 2002, my first marriage ended. Things had been shaky for some time, but I always felt that we would work things out. So it was a shock when my wife sat down one evening and said she didn't want to be married to me anymore. I moved out, rented a small apartment, became seriously depressed, and started drinking heavily.

For a while I blamed her for it all. In the previous couple of years, she'd gone back to school, made a whole new circle of younger friends, and spent most weekends socializing with them while I stayed home with our young son Jacob (a situation very similar to the family scenario in the early scenes of Pendulum Swings).

It took some time for me to realize that the blame wasn't all hers – that in fact, most of it may have been mine. We were both professing Christians when we married. A year later, we went to Bible school together, and after that we spent over a year working at our local church – teaching, running the youth program, and evangelizing our town. Our home was host to regular Bible studies and prayer meetings.

Then I returned to what I'd trained to do some years earlier: journalism. I established myself as a film critic for several publications, and began a popular column for my hometown newspaper, covering politics, sport, current events, and pretty much anything else that took my fancy. It also included music, particularly the local rock scene.

In a roundabout way, this led to working in the music industry itself and travelling the country with rock bands. This was not the wisest course I've followed in my life, and it wasn't long before I drifted into the worst of that lifestyle.

As I turned slowly away from God – and indeed, anything to do with Christianity – my wife stayed on course, the only Godly influence in our family, at least for a while. But eventually she was sucked into the rock 'n' roll life too, and she remained in it long after I'd left it behind. Among other things, her first year college project was a film documenting life on the road with a band.

This gradually took its toll on our marriage. It was a long time after the separation before I was able to admit to myself that although I was not entirely responsible for my wife's choices, our problems began with a series of bad decisions by me that ultimately led both of us away from the Lord.

It was some years before I got over that – before I could stop drinking, before I could look in the mirror without hating who I saw, before I stopped contemplating how much easier it would be just to end it all and before I was restored to healthy fellowship with Christ.

Sometimes I'm still plagued by guilt. I am especially haunted by the words of my son Jacob when he was seven years old and I was just a few months into separation. I was putting him to bed one night, tucking him in after his bedtime story, when he looked at me sadly and asked: "If I promise to be really good, do you think you and Mama and me could all live together again?"

I'd been blaming his mother. I'd been blaming myself. And meanwhile, our innocent boy was blaming himself for it all. My mistakes had scarred not only my own life but had horribly damaged my son's life, too.

Most of the time I can cling to Scripture, to what the Lord says about sin and guilt and forgiveness. But there are other times when I can't. Almost ten years down the road, this can still have a crippling effect on my life – and on the lives of those around me. It's what guilt can do. And on our own, we are no match for it.

Read today's relevant scripture, and see what God has to say about guilt.

Relevant Scripture

As a small group, take a few moments to read through today's scripture, and focus on reading these passages without thinking you already know what they are saying. Ask and allow the Spirit of God to guide you and your conversation. See where listening to the Spirit of God and some simple discussion takes you.

I John 1: 9

"If we confess our sins, He is faithful and just and will forgive us our sins and purify us from all unrighteousness."

Take some time now to think about this scripture. Pray and ask the Lord to help you understand what it means, and ponder on it alone before discussing your opinions and interpretations. Think about how this verse relates to guilt, and whether or not God's word lines up with our own feelings.

After you've spent some time considering this verse, discuss it together as a group. To help kick off the conversation, you may find it helpful to take a look at the Discussion Questions which follow next.

The discussion questions for today's small group study may help in understanding and discussing this passage of scripture. If discussion doesn't begin after the reading of the scripture, continue to the discussion questions.

Discussion Questions

"If we confess our sins, He is faithful and just and will forgive us our sins and purify us from all unrighteousness."

I John 1: 9

The book of 1 John makes it very clear that the true believer will not live a life of sin. This does not mean that the Christian will not sin at all (that's not what John is saying). He means that the daily walk of a true, genuine Christian will be marked by obedience to Christ and not by continued, habitual, sinful living.

But, as outlined in our scripture verse for today, the apostle declares that if and when we do sin, God has promised forgiveness and restoration. It is crucial that we grasp this, since forgiveness is so closely intertwined with how we deal with guilt.

This scripture raises some questions worth looking at:

- John says that when we confess our sins, and when God forgives us, he is being faithful. What do you think this means?
- There is a word in this verse that is often overlooked. That word is "just." In forgiving our sins, God is being just. That's right – justice is done! The judge of all the earth declares us "Not Guilty!" But how can that be?
- Since God declares the confessing sinner to be free of guilt, why do we continue to carry this great burden with us, often for years?
- Is there perhaps un-confessed sin that you need to deal with? If so, do you truly believe God when He says that He can and will forgive you?

Take plenty of time in this discussion and allow each other to be honest. Think through and brainstorm ways to make your gatherings more effective.

CHAPTER 11

Hiring Unbelievers

By Josh McDowell

Movie Connection

Show movie clip #11 on Group DVD

Barry approaches Dale offering him a job to help choose equipment for the new television and internet ministry at the church. Dale is depressed and negative about taking on the job. Barry makes the offer and leaves the door open for Dale to respond.

Discussion Starter Questions

- How much has Dale allowed his personal problems to bleed over into his professional life?
- Have the personal problems in Dale and Maria's marriage taken a toll on her professional life?
- Have you ever been in a position at work or in the ministry where you've had to hire or fire?
- Have you ever felt like God was leading you to do something that didn't line up with what was traditionally thought of as wisdom?
- Does a person's faith ever impact your hiring or firing decisions?

Life Connection

My Life Connection *by Josh McDowell*

I've had to hire and fire people in my work as a minister, and that's a tough situation. Every hiring and firing situation is tough, but for some reason it felt like a bigger issue when I was hiring and firing for the church and as a representative of God. Would God take away someone's source of income and risk placing them without a way of providing for their family? Would God ever choose someone who didn't have their life together and in some reasonable order? I can't say; I'm certainly not God.

Once upon a time, a man named Pastor White, in the heart of Tennessee, felt like God was telling him to hire a man to serve as a minister to young adults. But the Pastor couldn't comprehend this unusual feeling that seemed to be from God. See, the young man who Pastor White was considering hiring wasn't even an applicant; worse yet, the church was not looking for a minister to young adults (they didn't really have any young adults). Additionally, Jimmy, the young man on Pastor White's heart didn't even remotely look the part of a minister. Jimmy was a bartender at the local strip club in downtown Bristol, and Pastor White knew that Jimmy was struggling with his physical relationship with his girlfriend. Jimmy's language wasn't perfect either; he occasionally dropped a word considered vulgar here and there, even when he was at church. Jimmy was a young 32. I say that he was young because Jimmy still lived with and cared for his widowed mother. His demeanor was very quiet, and he rarely talked, except when he was asking questions of Pastor White or telling his friends at the bar about Jesus. This had recently become something that Jimmy was very passionate about.

It was clear to Pastor White that God was using Jimmy. Jimmy had talked to him about the relationship he had with his girlfriend and he wanted to remain pure. The problem here was that Monica had moved in with Jimmy and his mother. Monica and Jimmy had cared about one another for a good while, but their relationship only became physical on the day she moved in with him.

Let me tell you how this came to pass by going back a few months in the story. About six months prior to moving in with Jimmy, Monica got kicked out of her parent's house when she got pregnant from her now ex-boyfriend Nick. Later she lost the baby, but her parents never forgave her for ruining their reputation down at the church. So Monica moved in with her abusive boyfriend Nick, who may actually be responsible for causing her miscarriage. About 5 months ago, Monica began going to Jimmy's bar with Nick but continued to visit to talk to Jimmy long after Nick found another bar. (Abusive, angry, men like Nick are sometimes asked to find another place to drink if you understand what I'm saying). Anyway, Monica only moved in with Jimmy after her boyfriend beat her near the point of death for the last time. Jimmy considered killing Nick, but after gathering his gun and having a drink, he decided to stop by Pastor White's church.

Over the next few months, Jimmy talked to Pastor White as often as possible. Pastor White even stopped by the bar a few times risking his reputation as a Southern Baptist Pastor who taught against the dangers of alcohol, not to mention strip clubs. Because of a liquor license legality, Pastor White and any patrons of the bar could actually go in and out of the bar without ever seeing the stripers. (Lots of men claimed to love this bar just for the "bar side", and they were quick to explain to their wives that they never went over the strip club side). At the beginning, Pastor White would've gladly helped Jimmy find a different job but as time went on Pastor White saw the impact Jimmy was having on all of his friends. They were always in and out of the bar, they were always at Jimmy's house when Jimmy wasn't working and they were often asking Jimmy questions about Jesus. The stripers also noticed something different about Jimmy, it wasn't his language or his dress, and he dropped some profanity and dressed just like the others at the bar. Some were learning about Jesus and looking for other ways to support themselves, because Jimmy had convinced them that they were more valuable than objects of lust. Jimmy had convinced them that Jesus loved them and gave His life so that they could have a more abundant life than the life of a striper / prostitute. One day, after Pastor White's regular coffee and doughnut conversation with Jimmy at the church office, he couldn't help but pray for the stripers and many friends of Jimmy who were beginning to come toward a real relationship with Jesus Christ. As he prayed that day, he felt this overwhelming Spirit, voice, or direction from God about going before his congregation and asking them to pray over, anoint, and commission Jimmy as an apostle, minister, or "pastor" to those people he was sharing Jesus with. Pastor White didn't understand, he didn't have a full, clear vision and he knew that some members of the little community church would actually reject Pastor White for this idea, whether it was from God or not.

Pastor White was so confused. He didn't see how supporting Jimmy would help grow his church in any way. He didn't see his endorsement of Jimmy as anything but negative and controversial to his standing in the community. But he kept sensing from God that this wasn't about Pastor White or the "church" he was leading. This was about Jimmy and the confidence he needed to understand that God could and already was using him in a mighty way. Pastor White knew that Jimmy and Monica were "living in sin" by sharing a home and Jimmy even admitted to sharing a bed Monica. Was it possible that God was actually using Jimmy in-spite of his sin?

Of course the names and places within this story have been changed but the principle is there. What would you do if God spoke something to you that sounded totally out of line with traditional wisdom?

Hiring Unbelievers

Relevant Scripture

As a small group, take a few moments to read through today's scripture, and focus on reading these passages without thinking you already know what they are saying. Ask and allow the Spirit of God to guide you and your conversation. See where listening to the Spirit of God and some simple discussion takes you.

Genesis 22: 1-2

1 Now it came about after these things, that God tested Abraham,
and said to him, "Abraham!" And he said, "Here I am."
2 He said, "Take now your son, your only son, whom you love,
Isaac, and go to the land of Moriah, and offer him there as
a burnt offering on one of the mountains of which I will tell you."

Hosea 1:2

2 When the LORD first spoke through Hosea, the LORD said to Hosea, "Go, take to yourself a wife of harlotry and have children of harlotry; for the land commits flagrant harlotry, forsaking the LORD."

The discussion questions for today's small group study may help in understanding and discussing this passage of scripture. If discussion doesn't begin after the reading of the scripture, continue to the discussion questions.

Discussion Questions

"If we confess our sins, He is faithful and just and will forgive us our sins and purify us from all unrighteousness."

- How would you respond to God if He told you to sacrifice your child?
- How would you respond to God if you felt like He was leading you to do something that didn't seem to make good sense?
- Have you ever felt like God was telling you to do something that didn't seem very logical?
- Is it possible that God was really using Jimmy to minister to the people who regularly visited his bar?
- Could you even imagine a Christian working in a strip club? Some Christians believe drinking is wrong, but most if not all would recognize that striping isn't right in God's eyes.

Take plenty of time in this discussion and allow each other to be honest. Think through and brainstorm ways to make your gatherings more effective.

CHAPTER 12

Stiff Arming God

By Mary Reid

Movie Connection

Show movie clip #12 on Group DVD

Most of us have been where Dale was. We lived a season of life feeling like we had let God down and thinking that we were not on speaking terms with Him. We perceived God to have turned his back on us because of our failures and we lived according to those perceptions.

Discussion Starter Questions

- Has there ever been a time in your life that you could relate to Dale in this situation?
- Why did you think that you were not on speaking terms with God?
- What happened to change that?
- Looking back on it now, do you think that your perceptions of God lined up with reality?

Life Connection

My Life Connection *by Mary Reid*

When we feel like we don't measure up to God's standards it becomes easy to go days without speaking to Him. The days turn into weeks. The weeks turn into months. Before we know it years have passed us by and we find ourselves in a place where we feel like we are not on speaking terms with God. The problem is with our perception of reality and not with reality itself. Somewhere along the way we have been convinced of some things that are not true. Our sins, failures, and shame keep us from feeling worthy to approach God. In those intense moments of grief and anguish we don't even feel worthy to be called His child. For some reason we come to believe the lie that our behavior is capable of affecting the way that God feels about us. Then, once the lie takes us to that lonely place where we can no longer sense God, fear and guilt keep us there. As a man thinks in his heart so is he.

Somewhere along the way a false belief system has entered our heart. Somewhere along the way we were told what we needed to do in order to please God along with a lengthy list of what we should not do to keep from making Him mad. This false belief system sucks the life out of us and darkens our hearts. There was a time when I was in this place.

Back in 1998 I walked away from church with a warped perception of God, and a great sense of failure. I attended church for over two years and didn't experience any growth. I did all the things I was told to do but I still didn't experience life. I walked away, heartbroken, disappointed, defeated, and the only gain was that if I died I would go to heaven. (Truth be told I questioned that on most days). It would be another eight years before I would really get to know God. During those eight years I didn't pray, I didn't read my Bible, I didn't go to church, and I felt unworthy at best. I believed in the deepest parts of my being that God was disappointed in me, and this caused me to be incapable of having a relationship with Him.

While our perceptions have taken us to some strange places, reality hasn't changed at all. Nothing we do can change the way that God feels about us. He doesn't love us because we behave properly. He isn't crazy about us because we are so cool. He loves us because we are His children. He is crazy about us because we are His creation. Our reality, as a child of God, is dependent on Him not us. We can't mess it up no matter how hard we try.

God created humans for the purpose of relationship. He walked and talked with Adam and Eve in the Garden. They experienced God in a way that my mind can't comprehend. When Adam and Eve sinned in the Garden of Eden they bought into the same lie that is sold to us. Their response was the same as mine. They hid from God. All of a sudden their perceptions were twisted and a lie had darkened their heart. Even though God still loved them the same as He did before they sinned they could no longer comprehend that love.

We have been reconciled to God through Christ. That reality remains true despite the most twisted perceptions we may have. Standing on that truth we can approach God as His beloved. No matter what we have done or how long we have gone without talking to Him, He desires us to approach Him.

Jesus knew that we would be vulnerable to finding ourselves in this situation. He gave us three parables that express the heart of God to us when we find ourselves there.

Stiff Arming God

Relevant Scripture

As a small group, take a few moments to read through today's scripture, and focus on reading these passages without thinking you already know what they are saying. Ask and allow the Spirit of God to guide you and your conversation. See where listening to the Spirit of God and some simple discussion takes you.

Luke 15:1-7 "The Lost Sheep"

1 Now all the tax collectors and
the sinners were coming near Him to listen to Him.
2 Both the Pharisees and the scribes began
to grumble, saying, "This man receives sinners and eats with
them."
3 So He told them this parable, saying,
4 "What man among you, if he has a hundred sheep and
has lost one of them, does not leave the ninety-nine in
the open pasture and go after the one which
is lost until he finds it?
5 "When he has found it, he lays it on his shoulders, rejoicing.
6 "And when he comes home, he calls together his friends and
his neighbors, saying to them, 'Rejoice with me, for I
have found my sheep which was lost !'
7 "I tell you that in the same way, there will be more joy in
heaven over one sinner who repents than over ninety
nine righteous persons who need no persons repentance.

Luke 15 8-10 "The Lost Coin"

8 "Or what woman, if she has ten silver coins and loses one coin,
does not light a lamp and sweep the house and search carefully
until she finds it?
9 "When she has found it, she calls together her
friends and neighbors, saying, 'Rejoice with me, for I
have found the coin which I had lost!'
10 "In the same way, I tell you, there is joy in the presence of
the angels of God over
one sinner who repents."

Additional Reading

Luke 15 11-32 “The Prodigal Son”

The discussion questions for today's small group study may help in understanding and discussing this passage of scripture. If discussion doesn't begin after the reading of the scripture, continue to the discussion questions.

Discussion Questions

Turning us away from God is something Satan tries very hard to do. He has proven that he is excellent at it too. Do you ever wonder why some people are evil and have *everything* (well, in the world's eyes)? Then we see others go to church and have major life struggles. The answer is basic. If the Devil already has you in his grasp, then there is no reason to slam you. In some ways, we should be glad that we are tested. It means something good is around the corner. We just have to be careful not to let ourselves get in a position that stiff-arms God.

- How do you get back on speaking terms with God when you have given him the stiff-arm in the past?
- Would stiff-arming God be the same as no desire to pray?
- What are some of the excuses people use for pushing God away (whether they are intentional or not)?
- If we know of a friend who has been stiff-arming God, what are some things we could do or say to encourage them to look at their actions?

Take plenty of time in this discussion and allow each other to be honest. Think through and brainstorm ways to make your gatherings more effective.

CHAPTER 13

Earning Big in a Recession World

By Bob Templeton

Movie Connection

Show movie clip #13 on Group DVD

In the movie, Bobby meets Dale in the diner and starts to talk to him about how he is doing. Dale is really down and begins to wallow in his unfortunate circumstances. Bobby has done well in his life, both spiritually and financially. As the conversation turns from Dale's past to a possible brighter future, Bobby encourages Dale to earn his way out of the financial mess he is in by doing something he loves and is passionate about. One of the keys here is that if Dale spent his time on the things he is good at, he might be able to become his own boss and earn enough without having to work two or three jobs.

Bobby continues the conversation with an illustration of how a pendulum swings from side to side. Dale's life is on the bad side of the pendulum swing, and Bobby believes with some work and an attitude change things can swing back to the good side. Bobby doesn't stop with only financial advice; he continues to give spiritual advice concerning Dale's life. He mentions that even if Dale's life turned around financially, there would still be a void that wealth could not fill. The only solution to this life dilemma is a solid relationship with God. Bobby also says that his life is living evidence of what God can do for anybody willing to reach out to Him in faith.

Take some time to discuss the following questions, with openness and honesty. Remember, there can be more than one answer to the questions.

Discussion Starter Questions

- Is money considered good or evil?
- Are things of this world good or evil?
- Can money make you happy?
- Which do you believe is harder: poverty or extreme wealth? How do you really know?

Life Connection

My Life Connection *by Bob Templeton*

As of the writing of this chapter, I have not received a regular paycheck or unemployment check (churches don't pay unemployment tax) for 54 weeks.

When God led me to leave my position as a Christian school administrator, I was sure that I would go back into education or church work, and that what we were dealing with was only a temporary situation. I was wrong. Hey, I know many of you have gone through this or worse, but I have some great news! God is still in control and it is His desire to provide for the needs of His children. For us, this has been seen in several ways throughout this last year. We sold our home in a down market in less than 2 months, we cashed in a meager retirement that had recently taken an upturn, and God has used other people to bless us little by little on this journey.

The one thing that we must keep in focus during hard times is that God is not interested so much in what is happening to us as He is in what is happening in us. Dale was experiencing a difficult time but the purpose was bigger than the circumstance. Men, especially, suffer when they are not able to provide for their family like they should. This slams their ego and becomes a stronghold for the enemy to encourage doubt and depression. An independent soul is what keeps us from trusting in God. If we suffer and have to call out to God, Satan convinces us that we are weak and not worthy of our manhood.

In these uncertain economic times, we must trust in God and sometimes think outside the box as to ways to earn a living for us and our families. We live in amazing times. So much knowledge is available through the internet that can usually be accessed free through the local public library. Where, in years gone by, a person needed fifty thousand dollars just to start a brick and mortar business, today you can start a web-based business for less than $200. The key to success is knowledge and a God-given drive to change your life and boldly step out in faith.

I have learned also that sometimes it takes failure to lead to success. That failure is but a stepping stone to the success God has for you. Today we hear about the "prosperity gospel" but we don't hear that sometimes we'll fail over and over again prior to great success. It's been said that there are no "overnight" successes, only "overnight" recognition for the results of many failures. How would you like to present the following resume for a job:

> *Failed in business – bankruptcy / Defeated for legislature / Failed in business – bankruptcy a second time two years later / Fiancée died / Nervous breakdown / Defeated for US Congress / Defeated a second time for US Congress / Defeated for U.S. Senate / Defeated for Vice-President / Defeated for U.S. Senate a second time / Might should have quit but didn't - Oh yeah... elected President of the United States 1860 – Abraham Lincoln*

When we are rejected we many times feel like we've been personally attacked. It's a good thing Theodore Geisel didn't feel that way. He was rejected twenty-seven times before finding a publisher for his books written by his other name, "Dr. Seuss." Sometimes it takes time for God's plan to come together. Many times we give up too soon. The following NFL coaches share the record for having the worst first year records in professional football: Tom Landry, Chuck Noll, Bill Walsh, and Jimmy Johnson. They all only won a single game during the first season. However, if any of the clubs would have fired them after that first year, they would have missed out on their teams winning a Super Bowl (These four coaches accounted for eleven Super Bowl victories from 1974-1993).

The challenge is to take life step by step, day by day and follow the leading of the Holy Spirit. Dare to live a life of adventure and trust and be ready to act when God calls. We have been called to be Priests and Kings for the Kingdom God. Isn't it time we start acting like it?

Relevant Scripture

As a small group, take a few moments to read through today's scripture, and focus on reading these passages without thinking you already know what they are saying. Ask and allow the Spirit of God to guide you and your conversation. See where listening to the Spirit of God and some simple discussion takes you.

I Thessalonians 4:11-12

11and to make it your ambition to lead a quiet life and attend to
your own business and work with your hands, just as we
commanded you,
12so that you will behave properly toward outsiders and not be in
any need.

Matthew 5:16

16Let your light shine before men in such a way that they may see your good works, and glorify your Father who is in heaven.

Psalms 15:1-2

1O LORD, who may abide in Your tent?
Who may dwell on Your holy hill?
2He who walks with integrity, and works righteousness,
And speaks truth in his heart.

II Corinthians 9:7-12

7Each one must do just as he has purposed in his heart, not
grudgingly or under compulsion, for God loves a cheerful giver.
8And God is able to make all grace abound to you, so that always
having all sufficiency in everything, you may have an abundance
for every good deed;
9as it is written,

"HE SCATTERED ABROAD, HE GAVE TO THE POOR,
HIS RIGHTEOUSNESS ENDURES FOREVER."

10 Now He who supplies seed to the sower and bread for food will
supply and multiply your seed for sowing and increase the
harvest of your righteousness; 11 you will be enriched in
everything for all liberality, which through us is producing
thanksgiving to God. 12 For the ministry of this service is not only
fully supplying the needs of the saints, but is also overflowing
through many thanksgivings to God.

Additional Reading

I John 2:15-17

Luke 5:1-9

The discussion questions for today's small group study may help in understanding and discussing this passage of scripture. If discussion doesn't begin after the reading of the scripture, continue to the discussion questions.

Discussion Questions

- Why is it easier to trust God for our salvation than trust Him for our finances?
- Tell of a time when you had to put your trust in God rather than your job or abilities.
- How does *giving* help us in times of our own needs?
- How responsible are we to be as fellow believers when we know of other's needs and can meet them?
- How does an eternal perspective help us to love God over the things of this world?

Bonus:

- Challenge each of those in your group to be "someone else's" miracle this week.
- Discuss at least four things that stand in the way of us living the life of faith God wants for us?
- Compare the world's definition of success and your definition of success?

Take plenty of time in this discussion and allow each other to be honest. Think through and brainstorm ways to make your gatherings more effective.

CHAPTER 14

Revenge: Is It Worth It?

By Josh McDowell

Movie Connection

Show movie clip #14 on Group DVD

In the movie, we watch Dale get hit again and again by people in his life. At the end of the film, Dale has the opportunity to get revenge. He has the power in his hands to give back some of the exact persecutions that were delivered to him. In some ways, the audience says to give it to her, she deserves it. Others feel compassion; especially if they can see themselves in that position. Ultimately, we see what Dales decides to do.

Take some time to discuss the following questions, with openness and honesty.

Discussion Starter Questions

- Have you ever found yourself in Dale's position, with the opportunity to get back at someone?
- What would have been the result if Dale followed through with his opportunity for revenge?
- Who would have been affected by his decision for revenge?

Life Connection

My Life Connection *by Josh McDowell*

There is a story that I can't tell because it is so personal. I was treated badly, lied to, my livelihood was taken away, my family was embarrassed, my reputation was damaged, my children were confused and my personal confidence was so shaken that I considered walking away from the church all together.

While I was considering what to do, I read books. I read *The Ragamuffin Gospel, Blue like Jazz, So You don't want to go to Church Anymore, The Starfish and the Spider*, and *The Shack*. I prayed and cried out to God. I hurt. I wept. During that season, I would have taken revenge if I thought I could get away with it and if I could figure out exactly who to take it out on. I knew someone deserved my wrath, but I wasn't sure just who that someone was.

It took about two weeks for me to fully decompress, but after about two weeks I began to be so thankful for what had happened to me. It still wasn't right, I know now and I knew then that I had been done wrong. On the other hand, I was starting to realize that I had been guilty of evils of the same magnitude. When I say I was thankful for what had happened to me, I mean, I sat in my living room and cried my eyes out thanking God for my situation. I didn't know if I would have to work two or three jobs to get my life straightened out or if I would have to sell my house and downsize, but I knew that what was happening to me was GREAT.

I heard a story today about a mother who looked out her kitchen window to see her daughter in the back yard. The mother immediately dropped her dishes and ran to the little girl and began to beat her with all her strength. She hit the 3 year old on the head, back, stomach, arms and legs. She slapped her daughter to the ground and began kicking her over and over. Any onlooker from a distance would assume that this treatment was abusive. But the mother was beating the flames off her daughter's body. The mother's kicks were rolling her precious daughter on the ground to extinguish the flames. Looking back I wonder if what God allowed me to go through was His way of rescuing me from the flames of the lifestyle I was living.

I later had an opportunity to get revenge. One of the men who had contributed to my pain was in a situation almost identical to mine. I never even considered revenge at that point. Instead, I found myself deeply caring for him. My kind reaction wasn't due to my holiness, because in myself I have none. Instead, it was a natural response to the love God had given and worked in me.

Read today's relevant scripture, and see what God has to say about revenge.

Relevant Scripture

As a small group, take a few moments to read through today's scripture, and focus on reading these passages without thinking you already know what they are saying. Ask and allow the Spirit of God to guide you and your conversation. See where listening to the Spirit of God and some simple discussion takes you.

Paul, in his letter to the Romans, reminded them to "never pay back evil for evil to anyone." Take a moment and read this passage and discuss it briefly as a group:

Romans 12:17-21

17 Never pay back evil for evil to anyone. Respect what is right in the sight of all men.
18 If possible, so far as it depends on you, be at peace with all men.
19 Never take your own revenge, beloved, but leave room for the wrath of God, for it is written, "Vengeance is Mine, I will repay," says the Lord.
20 "but if your enemy is hungry, feed him, and if
he is thirsty, give him a drink; for in so doing you will heap burning coals on his head."
21 Do not be overcome by evil, but overcome evil with good.

Genesis 34

For additional study on the topic of revenge, read the story of Dinah.

Genesis 37

Another beautiful story about not exacting revenge is the story of Joseph in Genesis. Joseph's forgiveness and care for the brother's who sold him into slavery is an amazing picture of forgiveness.

Revenge: Is It Worth It?

The discussion questions for today's small group study may help in understanding and discussing this passage of scripture. If discussion doesn't begin after the reading of the scripture, continue to the discussion questions.

Revenge: Is It Worth It?

Discussion Questions

- Can someone share a time they wanted to get revenge? Did that revenge end the pain, or did it start a cycle of more revenge?

- Is revenge ever satisfying?

- When you are harboring hatred or anger, does it really hurt you or the one you are angry with?

- Dale gave Maria evidence at the end of the movie that could have resulted drastically in two separate ways. What would you have done differently?

- Is there someone you should forgive today?

Take plenty of time in this discussion and allow each other to be honest. Think through and brainstorm ways to make your gatherings more effective.

CHAPTER 15

Gossip

By Victor and Charity Gray

Movie Connection

Show movie clip #15 on Group DVD

"How *dare* she?"

I think that's the natural reaction that we have to the audacity that Tina displays when she confronts Dale about what she has *heard* about him. "Why are you such a liar" she asks. We can feel the shock that registers on Dale's face. She accuses him of being deceptive to his own children, of his financial hardships being a fabrication used to garner their sympathy, of not really wanting to spend time with them, of canceling plans for his own selfish agenda. Through all of this we've seen the truth. We *know* the truth. We have observed the behind-the-scenes. And so, of course we're equally disgusted with Dale's wife as we are with Tina. We know full well that Tina's accusations have ultimately come from Maria.

"It's horrible! It's disgusting! It's simply outrageous!"

I have to wonder why we feel so strongly about the kind of gossip that Dale endures. I think it's probably because we've all been there at some time, in some way. At some point, someone has made erroneous accusations about us, and we've felt the sting of those half-truths or out-right lies. We have been made to feel cheated, humiliated, and belittled. At the very least, Tina came to Dale with what she heard. More likely than not, we've been stabbed in the back instead of the front. We've also probably felt the frustration of knowing that once a lie has been spread about us, it is impossible to stop it. It's like an egg that's been cracked and poured out: There's no getting it back inside its fragile shell. True or not, what has been said has taken root in the psyche of those who have heard it, and there's no going back. It's easy to empathize with the victims of gossip. Though, it's hard to admit that we've been on the other end of a "juicy" story.

The truth is, we've all participated in that end as well. If we're honest, we can probably think of something recently, maybe last week or even yesterday, when we simply *had* to tell our spouse, friend, or relative what we heard about someone else. It feels like if we don't get it out, we're just going to *explode*. Besides, it's not going to go any further, right?

Somehow, gossip is a "Christian Sin." I know Bible-Believing-Born-Again-Children-of-God who would never *dream* of taking a drug, watching a porno, or having an abortion who don't think twice about circulating a nice spicy story about one of their friends, acquaintances, or neighbors! They probably preface their soap-opera tale with the classic cop-out, "I'm just telling you this so you can *pray* for them."

Take some time to discuss the following questions, with openness and honesty:

Discussion Starter Questions

- Have you ever found yourself in Tina's position because you were angry about something you heard?
- Do you think Tina was enjoying the verbal slapping she was giving Dale?
- Why do you think that people feel it's their right to address personal things to others in the way Tina did with Dale?
- Was Dale's stern reaction righteous anger or temper finally being let out?

Gossip

Life Connection

My Life Connection *by Victor and Charity Gray*

It sounds familiar: gossip. Because if I'm honest, I have to admit that I've "been there and done that." I have a feeling that you probably have too. And even though gossip is a common sin, it's still a sin. Sure, we've all done it at some point, but every single one of us has been *wrong* to do so.

When I was completing my last year of Bible school, I could tell that there was something wrong with the pastor of college ministries at my home church (a very large church that had an even greater reputation). I'll call him Chad. Chad didn't seem to have the same passion for reaching lost young people that he once had, especially when he first came to the church two years before. He didn't seem as interested in the lives of his students. He seemed to be rushing through his responsibilities at the church, "punching the clock" rather than being truly engaged. Attendance in the class, which had grown steadily since Chad came, had begun to drop greatly. I decided that I needed to confront him about the change I had seen in him. I was a twenty-two year old Bible student; so after all, I knew everything, and someone needed to set him straight! When I went to his office, Chad began to educate me on the real state of affairs, as a staff member of the church. The Executive Pastor of the church, who had been on staff for nearly thirty years and answered only to the Senior Pastor, was a hyper-conservative, dogmatic, despotic, egotistical tyrant who ran the church behind the scenes with an iron fist. And he had it out with Chad! He was jealous of the attention that he was getting. He hated that the college group had been growing and reaching new people with non-traditional ministry. He was even orchestrating the politics of the church to get the College Pastor fired! He was literally making up stories, gossiping about every aspect of Chad's life. "I have to deal with his attacks every single day," I remember him saying to me, somewhere between outrage and misery.

I felt horrible. I had it all wrong, and what I thought I had observed as distance and dissatisfaction in Chad was only the natural stress that would undoubtedly come when a snake like the executive pastor was working so hard against him.

It was because of this conversation that I wasn't surprised when my father came to me in my bedroom a few weeks later to tell me that Chad had left the church. "Why?" I demanded. My father was on the trustee-committee of the church, and as such found out information from the pastor that many people did not. "I really can't tell you," my dad said. "You don't have to," I replied hotly. I was close with Chad and devastated at his loss. "I know exactly who's at fault for him leaving," I told my father, then went on to recount the conversation Chad and I had in his office. I told him that I *knew* it was the Executive Pastor who ran him off, with all of his lies and gossip.

"That's not it," my dad told me.

I was so upset that I started weeping. I was crushed to think that the man who had done more to encourage me to live for Christ in a genuine love relationship had been silenced. I was so distraught that I just stayed in my room for several hours. Finally, my older sister came to consol me, or at least that's what I thought when she knocked my door. I told her as soon as she came in everything that I had learned, and how I believed that it was the Executive Pastor who had *driven* Chad away with his lies and deception."I have to tell you this," she said finally. "Chad didn't just leave the *church*. He *left the state* with a woman that's not his wife!"

I was in shock, but it was true. A call to Chad's wife confirmed what had happened. He had left the state with his wife's best friend. I had been dead wrong, no more so than about my assumptions of the Executive Pastor.

Gossip

The class that Chad normally taught, the one where attendance had fallen off, was packed to the rafters that Sunday. Everyone wanted to hear what had happened. Everyone was itching for the story.

Read today's relevant scripture, and see what God has to say about guilt.

Relevant Scripture

As a small group, take a few moments to read through today's scripture, and focus on reading these passages without thinking you already know what they are saying. Ask and allow the Spirit of God to guide you and your conversation. See where listening to the Spirit of God and some simple discussion takes you.

Proverbs 20:19

v19 He who goes about as a slanderer reveals secrets, Therefore do not associate with a gossip.

This verse gives us good advice: "He who goes about as a slanderer reveals secrets, therefore do not associate with a gossip." But what do we do when the gossip isn't coming from someone else? It's so hard not to build up our own injured egos with gossip. Ultimately, gossip is a matter of pride. We're likely to spread it because of pride. We like to hear stories of others' struggles because it makes us feel like our struggles are not as terrible by comparison. It can make us feel a lot better about our own struggling marriage when we hear about the affair that our co-worker is having. It makes us sigh with relief when we hear about a fellow church member's daughter getting pregnant, because our doubts about our own parenting must not be as bad. And if the *pastor* is being medicated for depression, well *hallelujah!* We must not be the terrible Christians who have trouble being joyful after all!

James 4:6

v6 But He gives a greater grace. Therefore it says, "God is opposed to the proud, but gives grace to the humble."

We know that pride is sinful. This verse tells us that "God is opposed to the proud." The original sin of Adam and Eve was a matter of pride, the desire for the knowledge of good and evil, to be as God Himself. That's why.

But I think we're also just as likely to allow gossip *about* us have a greater impact than what it should, because of pride. As we've already discussed, we've all probably been the victim of some form of gossip about something. The reason it stings so badly, the reason we can lose sleep over it, is actually a condition of pride. If we weren't concerned about what others thought about us, we wouldn't be bothered in the least. The truth is, if we correctly know the truth, it should be what is ultimately important to us. If we know that God is pleased with our actions, even if we have sinned and asked his forgiveness, other's opinions are inconsequential.

Ultimately, the struggle with gossip is the oldest struggle we have: the struggle against our own sinful pride. I believe that when we begin to realize our own great imperfection, that's when we'll begin to have victory over our own gossip problem.

The discussion questions for today's small group study may help in understanding and discussing this passage of scripture. If discussion doesn't begin after the reading of the scripture, continue to the discussion questions.

Discussion Questions

- In viewing pro's and con's of gossip, are there really any pro's at all?
- What are some ways that gossip is camouflaged?
- If we know someone is a constant source of gossip, how can we confront that person without gossiping ourselves?
- If we heard about a situation that hits close to home, how can we help the situation without crossing the gossip line?
- Has someone ever gossiped about you or your family? How would you address the situation?

Take plenty of time in this discussion and allow each other to be honest. Think through and brainstorm ways to make your gatherings more effective.

CHAPTER 16

Alcohol

By Robbie Starnes

Alcohol

Movie Connection

Show movie clips #16 on Group DVD

(Alcohol Segment -1)

Dale went from drinking tea to ordering a beer. In the scene, he orders tea out of habit but then calls the waitress back and orders a beer. This is where it begins.

(Alcohol Segment -2)

In this scene, we see Dale struggle with whether to get the hard liquor out of the cabinet or to leave it. After a bitter discussion about the money he owes, he reaches for a beer in the refrigerator but then turns and goes for the hard liquor in the cabinet. This time he slams the cabinet door shut.

(Alcohol Segment -3)

Finally he is alone and drinking in a deep pit of self inflected despair.

Drinking obviously is affecting his life. For Dale, it isn't just a casual beer with his lunch. It becomes something that grips his life in a negative way. Not all of Dale's problems are because of being drunk, but being drunk has degraded his life. Eventually, he makes a conscious decision that he's going to change. This is represented by pouring his beer down the drain and cleaning himself up.

It isn't addressed in the film, but not everyone can pour the bottle out and move on. For some, it takes a lifelong effort to stay sober and avoid the pitfalls of alcohol abuse.

Alcohol

Take some time to discuss the following questions, with openness and honesty. There are many different opinions on general drinking. What we want to focus on is abuse.

Discussion Starter Questions

- How does alcoholism impact our society today?
- Do you think Dale realizes the impacts of alcohol in his life from the beginning?
- Do you think that the night out to the bars with Maria and her friends had any effect on Dale's decision to start drinking later in the film?
- Why do you think Dale was struggling so much with the transition from tea to beer to liquor?

Alcohol

Life Connection

My Life Connection *by Robbie Starnes*

The use of alcohol is a key theme throughout *Pendulum Swings*. In the beginning, Maria and her friends are having a good time at a night club. These good times with her friends seem to make better memories than her home life with her husband. Maria's marriage, like her drink, is on the rocks.

Later, after the marriage is over, Dale sits alone at a diner and orders a beer. His use of alcohol from that point on increased. And so did his troubles. The old saying, "first the man takes a drink, then the drink takes a drink, then the drink takes the man," is evident in Dale's life. From the first drink that Dale takes to the drink that takes Dale, the consequences of alcohol abuse are a key theme in the film.

Every culture, past and present, has experienced the use and abuse of alcohol. In our culture, mainline denominational teaching regarding the use of alcohol is as wide as the pendulum's swing, from strict abstinence to moderation. From Jesus' turning the water into wine to how Christians celebrate communion, our personal convictions are mostly determined by the church we attend.

It would be easy to get into a debate in tonight's small group about exactly where we should stand on the subject of alcohol, but I think it would be much more valuable for us to consider what may be a better use of our time. Maybe the debate shouldn't be about the use of alcohol; instead, how we can minister to those in the trap of alcoholism.

Should we support an AA group by providing them a place to meet? Should we start a "Christian" 12 step group like Celebrate Recovery?

It would be easy for a small group to take some time and discuss the dangers, evils, or symptoms of alcohol, but instead let's take a few moments tonight and think on the positives of Ephesians 5:15-21, rather than the admonition not to be drunk with wine. Can we engage in the *positives*, such as taking care of how we walk, using our time wisely, and being filled with the Spirit?

Read today's relevant scripture, and see what God has to say about alcohol.

Alcohol

Relevant Scripture

As a small group, take a few moments to read through today's scripture, and focus on reading these passages without thinking you already know what they are saying. Ask and allow the Spirit of God to guide you and your conversation. See where listening to the Spirit of God and some simple discussion takes you.

Ephesians 5:15-21

15"Therefore be careful how you walk, not as unwise men but
as wise,
16 making the most of your time, because the days are evil.
17So then do not be foolish, but understand what the will of
the Lord is.
18And do not get drunk with wine, for that is dissipation, but
be filled with the Spirit,
19speaking to one another in psalms and hymns and spiritual
songs, singing and making melody with your heart to the Lord;
20always giving thanks for all things in the name of
our Lord Jesus Christ to God, even the Father;
21and be subject to one another in the fear of Christ.

The discussion questions for today's small group study may help in understanding and discussing this passage of scripture. If discussion doesn't begin after the reading of the scripture, continue to the discussion questions.

Alcohol

Discussion Questions

- How do you confront someone who is drunk most of the time and you see it affecting their life? What do you think would help them to listen?

- If your husband or wife has gradually progressed to alcohol abuse, what measures do we take to address the situation without damaging the relationship?

- What are other things in our lives, other than drugs, that can become addicting and as damaging as alcoholism?

- What do you think it means in Ephesians 5, where it says walk in the Spirit?

- Can you give an example of a time you were walking in the Spirit or a time that you obviously weren't walking in the Spirit?

- Read slowly through today's scripture and ask one another this question: Are we living the positives in this passage or just working hard to avoid the negative of being drunk with wine?

Take plenty of time in this discussion and allow each other to be honest. Think through and brainstorm ways to make your gatherings more effective.

Acknowledgements

Being the Executive Producer and Director of the film Pendulum Swings, a lot of credit is pushed my way. In reality, credit needs to go to the many people who gave of their time and talents for what has turned out to be a great journey in film. It is one thing to have a single responsibility. It is another thing to have multiple responsibilities. Many had those important jobs and performed them well. I am proud of our team.

One of the many ventures beyond the film was the music. There are too many names to mention but collectively, the group did a magnificent job. We had the ability to create tailored orchestrations that made scenes in the film come alive with fullness of sound. We had beautiful multi-track recordings from the orchestra at Immanuel Bible Church in Virginia. All together this was another team that worked tirelessly to provide for us a high quality of music.

I am very thankful for the writers, organizers and editors of this Bible study. The long hours put into each subject were definitely a gift from the heart. I came to Josh and proposed the idea of writing a Bible study that would focus on key biblical points from the film. Without hesitation, Josh ran with the concept. Josh studied the script and came up with 16 titles that are presented in the book. Then he researched and found 10 writers, including himself, to tackle the subjects from Pendulum Swings. These 10 writers have written from their heart and from personal experiences they have encountered in their lives. We were greatly blessed to have had them work with us in the creation of this Bible study.

Bill Rahn
Executive Producer/Director
PENDULUM SWINGS